This book belongs to

. . . .

. . . .

LONDON, NEW YORK, SYDNEY, PARIS,
MUNICH, and JOHANNESBURG

Written in consultation with child psychologist
Flora Hogman, Ph.D.
Senior Editor Linda Esposito
U.S. Editor Beth Sutinis
Senior Art Editor Sonia Whillock
Production Silvia La Greca
Jacket Design Victoria Harvey
Medical Consultant Dr. Susan Davidson

First American Edition, 2001
Published in the United States by DK Publishing, Inc.
95 Madison Avenue, New York, NY 10016

2 4 6 8 10 9 7 5 3 1

Library of Congress Cataloging-in-Publication Data

Robbins, Beth.
Tom and Ally visit the doctor / by Beth Robbins ; illustrated by Jon Stuart.--1st American ed.
p. cm. -- (It's O.K.)
Summary: When cat siblings, Tom and Ally, visit the doctor for a check-up,
Tom is scared of receiving a shot, but soon realizes that there is nothing to fear.
ISBN 0-7894-7429-8 -- ISBN 0-7894-7428-X (pbk.)
[1. Medical care--Fiction. 2. Physicians--Fiction. 3. Fear--Fiction. 4. Cats--Fiction]
Animals--Fiction.] I. Stuart, Jon, ill. II. Title. III. Series.

PZ7.R53235 Ne2001
[E]--dc21   00-058938

Color reproduction by Colourscan, Singapore
Printed and bound by L.E.G.O. in Italy

see our complete
catalog at
www.dk.com

IT'S OK!

Tom and Ally Visit the DOCTOR!

BY BETH ROBBINS

ILLUSTRATED BY JON STUART

DK Publishing, Inc.

"I finished my breakfast," said Tom.
"Can I go out to play?"

"Not this morning," said Mom.
"You and Ally are going to the doctor for a checkup,
remember? We talked about it yesterday."

"The doctor is going to check
that we're O.K." said Tom.
"That's right," said Mom.

"Are we going to get shots?" asked Ally.
"Shots? What are shots?" asked Tom.
"They stick a needle in your arm," said Ally.

Mom gave Ally a look.

But it was too late.

5

"A needle!" squealed Tom.
"I don't want a needle in my arm!"
He started to cry.

"Doctor Little is very gentle," said Mom.
"You'll hardly feel a thing.
It's just a little sting."

Tom stopped crying,
but he was still scared.

Ally was upset that Tom
was getting all the attention.
"I don't want a shot, either!" she wailed.

Dad tried to reassure the kittens.
"I've had plenty of shots," he said.
"And they don't
bother me
one little bit."

"The problem is that you *think* the shot will hurt," said Dad.
"But if you think about something else,
it's over in a flash!" he said,
snapping his fingers.

After breakfast, Dad waved them off.

"Why aren't you coming?" asked Ally.
"I've got too much gardening to do," said Dad.
"But when you come home, you can have
a bowl of strawberries, fresh from the garden!"

Tom and Ally loved strawberries.

The waiting room at the doctor's office was busy.

MIMI
LITTLE, M.D.

Mom said hello to everyone she knew.

"Which twin is this?" she asked Mr. Burrows.
"I wish I knew," he said.
"I heard them arguing and found this!"
A muffled noise came
from under the bucket.

"The other one must
have hopped it!"
Mom laughed.

"And what happened to Paddy?" asked Mom.
"He was playing leapfrog," said Mrs. Hopper.
"He jumped too high and hit the ceiling."

"Ouch!" said Mom. "Poor Paddy!"
"Yes, but he shouldn't
have been showing off,"
said Mrs. Hopper.

Mrs. Cluck fluttered over for a chat.

"Oh, dear," said Mom.
"Your little ones don't look well."

"They're not," said Mrs. Cluck.
"You should keep your kittens away.
I think it's chicken pox."

"It's better if they get it
when they're young," said Mom.
"It's much worse for grown-ups."

Mrs. Cluck clucked in agreement.
"When I was a chick,
people held chicken pox parties
so the kids would catch it
on purpose!"

The kittens could hardly
believe their ears.
A chicken pox party?
Yuck!

"Can we play over there?" asked Ally.

There was a play area full of books and toys.
It was far away from the chicks and their spots.

"Yes, of course," Mom smiled.

Paddy came to play with them, too.
But he didn't want to play
any jumping games.

They were having so much fun
that Tom and Ally forgot
all about their shots.

17

The line to see Doctor Little got shorter and shorter.

When Ally turned to look for the chicks, they had already left.

Mr. Burrows went in

and came out with—Flop!

Flop's floppy ear was the only way to tell the twins apart.
Flop was hopping mad.
"When I find Flip, he's going to be sorry he put that bucket on my head!" he said.

Paddy was the next to go in.
He came out wearing a bandage.

"How's your head?" asked Ally.
"Doctor Little said it'll be fine," said Paddy.

"Let's hope you've knocked some
common sense into it!" said Mrs. Hopper.

"Tom and Ally Katt, come in, please."

When Doctor Little called their names, Tom remembered the shot.

Mom came in with them
and sat on a chair.

Doctor Little was very friendly.
"I'm going to check
you both over," she smiled.

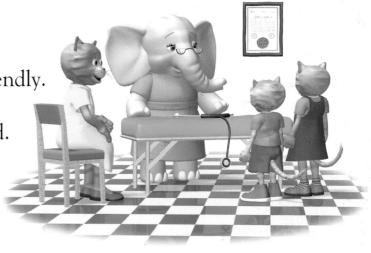

First the doctor weighed them

and measured them.

"Do you know what this is?"
asked Doctor Little.
"A trunk," said Tom.
"No, this instrument!"
The doctor laughed.
Tom shook his head.

"It's a stethoscope," she said.
"It helps me hear
what's going on inside you."

The doctor listened to their chests.
"Take some deep breaths
in and out," she said.

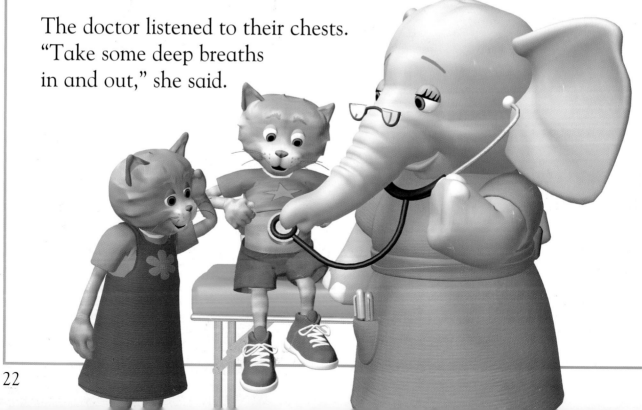

She listened to their hearts.
"Very good," she said.

Then she let Tom and Ally
listen to each other's heart.

Tom was amazed.
Ally's heart sounded
like a beating drum.
"It's so loud," he said.

Next Doctor Little checked
how well they could see.

She pointed to letters on a card.
The kittens had to point
to the same letters on their own cards.

The letters started off big
and ended up small.

After that, Doctor Little
checked their hearing
by standing behind them
and whispering.

"This way you can't
read my lips,"
she whispered to Tom.

Next she looked into their mouths and eyes and ears
with instruments that had little flashlights on the ends.

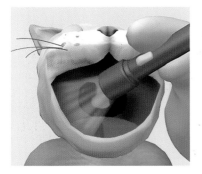  

"What clean ears you have!" said Doctor Little.
Mom looked proud.

Then the doctor lay them on a bed
and felt their tummies.

"Can you feel what I had
for breakfast?" asked Tom.

"I can feel it was a big one!"
Doctor Little laughed.

Finally, she made some notes
and smiled at the kittens.
"You're both in perfect health!"
she said.

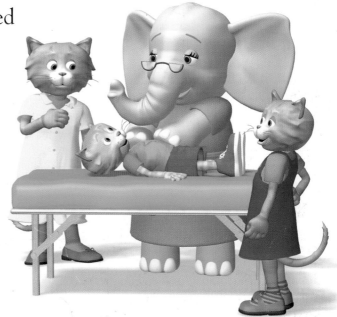

"If we're in perfect health, why do we need shots?" asked Ally.

"I don't like needles," whispered Tom.

Doctor Little put her arms around the kittens. "You need your shots so you'll *stay* healthy. They keep you from getting sick."

Doctor Little patted Ally's head. "Let's show Tom there's nothing to worry about."

When Doctor Little picked up the syringe, Tom looked away.

When he looked back, Ally was smiling. "It didn't hurt at all!" she said.

Tom closed his eyes
and tried to think of strawberries.
Then he felt . . . a little sting.

"All finished!" said Doctor Little.
Tom couldn't believe it!

Doctor Little gave Tom and Ally
gold stars for being brave.

"I'm so proud of my kittens," said Mom
as they waved good-bye to the doctor.

When they got home,
there were two bowls of strawberries
and a pitcher of milk on the kitchen table.

Just as the kittens started eating,
Dad came limping in from the garden.

"What happened?" asked Mom.
"I was digging the new flower beds
and I stepped on a rake!"

"We'll have to take you to
the doctor!" said Ally.
"Doctor Little is really nice," said Tom.
"She'll make you better."

Doctor Little laughed to see them again so soon.
She cleaned up Dad's foot and bandaged it.

"It's a nasty cut," said the doctor.
"I'd better give you a tetanus shot,
in case you got germs in it."

Dad didn't look too happy about that.

Mom took the kittens by the hand.
"Let's wait outside. It's a little crowded in here."

"Don't worry," said Ally. "It won't hurt too much."

"Think about something nice," said Tom.
"It will be over in a flash!"

When Dad came out, he was smiling.

"Look!" said Tom. "Dad has a gold star."
"Good for you!" said Ally. "When we get home
you can have a big bowl of strawberries!"